MEAN MACHINES

SUPERBIKES

130 150

90 100

80

70

60

50

40

30

PAUL HARRISON

W

Bromley Libraries

30128 80160 374 0

KU-515-822

This paperback edition published in 2014

First published in 2012 by Franklin Watts

Copyright © 2012 Arcturus Publishing Limited

Franklin Watts
338 Euston Road
London NW1 3BH

Franklin Watts Australia
Level 17/207 Kent Street, Sydney NSW 2000

Produced by Arcturus Publishing Limited,
26/27 Bickels Yard, 151–153 Bermondsey Street, London SE1 3HA

The right of Paul Harrison to be identified as the author of this work has been asserted by him in accordance with the Copyright, Designs and Patents Act 1988.

All rights reserved.

Text: Paul Harrison
Editor: Joe Harris
Design: sprout.uk.com
Cover design: sprout.uk.com

Picture credits:
Corbis: 8 (Rebecca Cook/Reuters), 11 (Leo Mason), 12 (Cezaro De Luca/epa/Corbis). David Katz: 9t, 9b. David Wilkinson/Offside: 20t, 20b, 21b. Ecosse Moto Work, Inc: 14–15. Honda Motor Europe Ltd: 26, 27t, 27b. Icon Sheene: 6–7. Kassander der Minoer: 21t. Marine Turbine Technologies LLC: front cover br, 22, 23t, 23b. Motorcycles-USA.com/Bart Madson: 10t, 10b. Ncrfactory: 18, 19. Rewaco Trikes: 30–31. Shaw Harley-Davidson: 28–29. Shutterstock: front cover l and tr, 1, 3. Suzuki GB PLC: 13t, 13b, 24–25. Yamaha-motor.co.uk: 16–17c, 17t. Tim Keeton/Impact Images: 4, 5t, 5b.

A CIP catalogue record for this book is available from the British Library.

Dewey Decimal Classification Number 629.2'275

ISBN 978 1 4451 3113 9

Printed in China

Franklin Watts is a division of Hachette Children's Books, an Hachette UK company.
www.hachette.co.uk

SL002134EN
Supplier 03, Date 1113, Print Run 3052

CONTENTS

MV-AUGUSTA F4CC

What makes a superbike 'super'? The motorcycles in this book have been taken to the extreme. They are faster, more expensive, more striking and more exclusive than any ordinary bike. One of the rarest and most expensive bikes around today is the MV-Augusta F4CC.

The F4CC is based on Augusta's F4R. However, over 90% of the parts for the F4CC were made specially for it.

The F4CC uses brakes that are usually found on racing motorbikes.

The F4CC is very exclusive. Only 100 of them were made.

The Italian firm MV-Augusta have been making racing motorbikes since 1954. The sporty F4CC continues on that path. The 'CC' in its name is the initials of the managing director of the firm, Claudio Castiglioni. He wanted to make a bike that he was proud to put his name to – the F4CC is the result of that dream.

The speed is limited to 315 km/h (195 mph) to protect the tyres from ripping apart.

The F4CC is made of light but strong materials, including titanium and carbon fibre.

SUPER STATS

MV-AUGUSTA F4CC
TOP SPEED: 315 km/h (195 mph)
WEIGHT: 187 kg (412.3 lbs)
ENGINE: 200 bhp
MADE IN: Italy
PRICE: £78,000

There are six gears – but you can travel at over 129 km/h (80 mph) in first!

ICON SHEENE

Superbikes often look like vehicles from the future. However, one of the rarest and most expensive superbikes has an old-fashioned styling – and the makers have done this on purpose. It is called the Icon Sheene, and it's the perfect mix of old and new.

Each Icon Sheene is built by hand. The fuel tank alone takes over a month to make.

Owners can buy an exclusive helmet to go with the bike. It will be painted by the same man who painted Barry Sheene's helmets.

The engine comes from the Japanese company Suzuki.

There is a painting of a playing card on each bike. Each painting is different and is of one of the 52 cards you get in a packet of playing cards.

The Icon Sheene takes its name from the British motorbike racing legend, Barry Sheene. The motorbike has been made as a tribute to him. For that reason, it looks a lot like the bikes Sheene raced on. Even the way the engines are powered is similar.

The Icon Sheene is highly exclusive – only 52 will be made. This is because Barry Sheene was 52 when he died.

SUPER STATS

ICON SHEENE
TOP SPEED: 322 km/h (200 mph)
WEIGHT: 200 kg (440 lbs)
ENGINE: 257 bhp
MADE IN: Great Britain
PRICE: £107,000

The Icon Sheene has a turbo-charged engine. Turbo chargers squeeze more air into an engine to give it more power.

MEAN MACHINES

DODGE TOMAHAWK

A superbike should be eye-catching – and no bike causes more double-takes than the Dodge Tomahawk. It may be one of the strangest looking superbikes around, but it is also one of the fastest.

The engine is five times more powerful than that in a small family car.

The Tomahawk is made from aluminium, which is very light and very strong.

The American firm Dodge is famous for making cars and trucks, not bikes. That might explain the Dodge Tomahawk's odd looks. It's got four wheels like a car, not two wheels like a normal motorbike. Even the engine comes from a car – a super sports car also made by Dodge, called the Viper.

The Tomahawk may look great, but it is not legal to drive it on the road.

The wheels are grouped in two batches of two.

The engine sends the power to the two rear wheels.

The Tomahawk is a concept bike. That means it was never meant to be made in any great number. Instead it shows what could be possible in the future.

SUPER STATS

DODGE TOMAHAWK

TOP SPEED: estimated 483+ km/h (300+ mph)

WEIGHT: 680 kg (1500 lbs)

ENGINE: 500 bhp

MADE IN: USA

PRICE: £353,000

MEAN MACHINES

TOP 1 ACK ATTACK STREAMLINER

Some motorbikes are built purely for speed. The Ack Attack is designed to break records, while drag bikes go head-to-head in the fastest bike races on Earth.

Ack Attack has reached a top speed of an incredible 634 km/h (394 mph).

Ack Attack is built around two Suzuki Hayabusa engines (see pages 24-25).

The fastest motorbike in the world is called Top 1 Ack Attack. It is a type of bike called a streamliner. Streamliners have a completely enclosed body. This allows the air to pass around the bike more smoothly.

Ack Attack needs a parachute to help it slow down.

DRAG BIKES

Drag bikes can accelerate to 161 km/h (100 mph) in 1.1 seconds.

The fastest sports motorbikes on the planet are drag bikes. They compete in races along straight, quarter-mile (400 m) tracks. Some of them run on a special fuel called nitromethane.

A big wheel at the back of the bike provides lots of grip.

Some drag bikes have a long metal frame at the back called a wheelie bar. This stops the bike from tipping backwards.

SUPER STATS

TOP 1 ACK ATTACK STREAMLINER
TOP SPEED: 634 km/h (394 mph)
WEIGHT: 907 kg (2000 lbs)
ENGINE: 1100 bhp
MADE IN: USA
PRICE: Not for sale

KTM 690 RALLY

Most superbikes are designed for tearing around on a road or race track. However, some are built for much tougher terrain. Going off-road is a real test of how durable a bike can be. These superbikes show just how it should be done.

The strong chassis stays rigid. This makes the KTM 690 easier to drive at high speed on rough surfaces.

The KTM 690 Rally has six gears.

The KTM 690 is a purebred rally bike. It was designed to compete in some of the longest, toughest races in the world. The most famous is the Dakar Rally, a gruelling all-terrain race which can be over 8,000 km (5,000 miles) long. No problem for the KTM, though – it won the event three years in a row.

Suspension helps to smooth at bumps. The KTM hits some big bumps, so the suspension can move up and down by 300 mm (12 inches).

SUZUKI RM-Z450

Motocross racing sees bikes competing against each other on off-road courses. Sometimes these can be purpose-built indoor tracks, but the more powerful bikes race outdoors. One of the best motocross superbikes is the Japanese-made Suzuki RM-Z450.

Big knobbly tyres help off-road bikes to grip slippery surfaces.

Off-road bikes sit higher above the ground than road bikes. This is to stop them scraping against bumpy ground.

Some motocross bikes are as loud as a jet plane coming in to land!

SUPER STATS

KTM 690 RALLY
TOP SPEED: 177 km/h (110+ mph)
WEIGHT: 162 kg (357 lbs)
ENGINE: 72 bhp
MADE IN: Austria
PRICE: Not for sale

ECOSSE TITANIUM SERIES

If superbikes are meant to be exotic, then the Ecosse Titanium may be the most super of all. This American-made speed machine has been constructed from some of the most expensive materials on earth. For a while, the Titanium was the costliest bike that money could buy. A newer version, called the FE Ti XX, sells for £192,000!

On the Ecosse even the exhaust pipe is made from titanium.

Titanium is a very difficult metal to weld, so extra care has been taken when making the Titanium series.

Each bike is individually numbered.

Titanium is a very expensive metal. Instead of painting it, Ecosse have hand-polished the titanium to show it off.

The suspension is up to Moto GP standard.

Although the Titaniums are amazing bikes, they are actually based on an older Ecosse model called the Heretic. This doesn't mean that the Titaniums have been easy to make. It actually took eighteen months of researching, designing and testing before the bikes were ready.

It's no surprise that the Titaniums are fast – the engines have been developed with a firm that builds drag bikes.

SUPER STATS

ECOSSE TITANIUM
TOP SPEED: Not known
WEIGHT: 200 kg (440 lbs)
ENGINE: 200+ bhp
MADE IN: USA
PRICE: £176,000

MOTO GP

The people who make motorbikes try lots of different ways of advertising their bikes. One popular way is through motorbike racing. Manufacturers hope that if their bikes do well in races, people may want to buy their machines. The two biggest forms of motorbike racing are called Moto GP and World Superbikes.

The engines of the bikes can be up to 800 cc. The cc stands for cubic capacity and shows the the size of the cylinders.

Light, powerful bikes are very fast. Moto GP rules state that its bikes have to have a minimum weight of 150 kg (330 lbs).

The form of bike racing that is closest to Formula 1 car racing is called Moto GP. This is where the biggest bikes compete against each other. These aren't bikes that you can buy in any showroom. They are specially built just to compete in GP races and use the most up-to-date technology to make them as fast as possible.

Bikes like the Yamaha YZR-M1 are designed for race tracks and can't be ridden on public roads.

Riders lean forward into a streamlined position.

The Yamaha YZR-M1 has lightweight carbon brakes on the front wheels.

The wheels are made of magnesium, which is both light and strong.

SUPER STATS

YAMAHA YZR-M1
TOP SPEED: 320+ km/h (200+ mph)
WEIGHT: 150 kg (330 lbs)
ENGINE: 200+ bhp
MADE IN: Japan
PRICE: Not for sale

NCR M16

The wheels are made from carbon fibre, which is light and strong.

The engine covers are made from titanium.

The Italian bike firm NCR create custom-built dream machines – at a price many of us can only dream of. Each of their bikes is hand-made, with an attention to detail that would put watchmakers to shame. They are meant to be the world's most exclusive bikes.

The original steel frame has been replaced by a carbon fibre one.

The disc brakes on the wheels are ceramic rather than metal. Ceramic brakes do not overheat like metal ones.

All the aluminium used in the bike is of the same standard as that used in aircraft.

What NCR have done is take a replica Moto GP bike from another Italian bike manufacturer and make it even more amazing. The original bike was called the Ducatti Desmosedici RR. NCR have stripped it down and tuned it up. It's now a leaner, meaner, faster machine.

The M16 is only made on request.

The covers at the front of the bike are called fairings. The M16's fairings have been cut away to save weight.

The NCR has six gears.

SUPER STATS

NCR M16
TOP SPEED: Not released
WEIGHT: 145 kg (319 lbs)
ENGINE: 200+ bhp
MADE IN: Italy
PRICE: £100,000 (estimated) and £140,000 for the Ducatti Desmosedici RR

JAWA RACERS

Superbikes don't have to be jaw-droppingly powerful and expensive to give their riders maximum thrills. Some of the fastest bikes around are actually very basic. These lightweight machines compete in races where speed and nerves of steel go hand-in-hand.

Like all other speedway bikes, the Jawa has only one gear.

Speedway bikes don't have brakes!

One of the lightest, quickest racing bikes is the Jawa 889 speedway bike. Speedway racing sees four riders racing against each other round an oval track. The track is around 300 metres (984 ft) long and each four-lap race lasts for around a minute. The track surfaces are made from a loose material such as shale brick granules.

Jawa bikes also race in another competition that is very similar to speedway. There's just one major difference – the races take place on ice. The bikes used are like speedway bikes, but have some special modifications.

Ice racers have spiked tyres to get a better grip on the ice. The spikes are made from metal and screw into the tyres.

The Jawa accelerates to 100 km/h (62 mph) in about 3 seconds – that's nearly as fast as a Formula 1 race car.

The Jawa uses a fuel called methanol. This allows the engine to produce more power than petrol would.

SUPER STATS

JAWA 889
TOP SPEED: 110+ km/h (70+ mph)
WEIGHT: 80 kg (176 lbs)
ENGINE: 68 bhp
MADE IN: Czech Republic
PRICE: £4,600

MTT TURBINE SUPERBIKE

Superbike makers have tried lots of tricks to make their bikes go faster. New materials are used to make the bikes lighter. Different fuels have been tried to make the engines more powerful. But a manufacturer called MTT has done something remarkable. It has made a superbike with a completely different sort of engine – a turbine. Or what you and I would call a jet engine!

This is the fastest production bike in the world.

The turbine engine is made by Rolls Royce.

These fairings are made from carbon fibre.

MEAN MACHINES

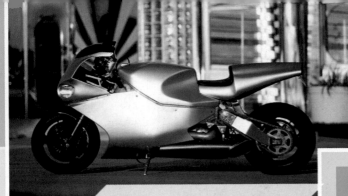

The Superbike once raced – and beat – a jet plane over a 1.6-km (one-mile) track.

The engine can run on diesel, kerosene or aviation fuel.

MTT don't usually make bikes – they make custom-built, turbine-powered machines such as air boats and pumps. Turbine engines use high-speed compressed air and fuel to generate their power – and they can produce a lot of power. The engine in the MTT Superbike is often found in helicopters!

The frame of the Superbike is made from aluminium.

Y2K

You've got to be patient to get your hands on one of these jet-powered marvels. They can take up to 12 weeks to build.

SUPER STATS

MTT TURBINE SUPERBIKE
TOP SPEED: 365 km/h (227 mph)
WEIGHT: 226 kg (500 lbs)
ENGINE: 320 bhp
MADE IN: USA
PRICE: £112,000

MEAN MACHINES

SUZUKI HAYABUSA

Many of the bikes in this book cost over £100,000 – and for that money, you'd expect something impressive. However, you don't have to spend that much to get a bike with a beast of an engine. One tenth of that cost will buy you a Suzuki Hayabasa – the most powerful production bike in the world.

The Hayabusa is blisteringly quick. It gets from 0-100 km/h (0-62 mph) in 2.7 seconds. It hits top speed in just over 18 seconds.

The Hayabusa's top speed is limited to 299 km/h (186 mph) for safety reasons. The bike could actually go quicker than this.

Hayabusas are famously reliable, and are known for not breaking down very often.

The world's fastest motorbike, the Ack Attack Streamliner (see pages 10-11) uses Hayabusa engines. That's how good they are!

The Suzuki Hayabusa has been in production since 1999. The name Hayabusa is actually Japanese for 'peregrine falcon'. It's a fitting name, as the peregrine is the fastest creature on the planet. It can reach speeds of over 322 km/h (200 mph) when it dives to catch its prey.

Two lights are better than one. The Hayabusa has twin headlights at the front, mounted one above the other.

SUPER STATS

SUZUKI HAYABUSA
TOP SPEED: 299 km/h (186 mph)
WEIGHT: 260 kg (573 lbs)
ENGINE: 194 bhp
MADE IN: Japan
PRICE: £10,935

The inside of the front suspension fork is coated with a diamond-like substance. This helps the inner tubes move up and down more smoothly.

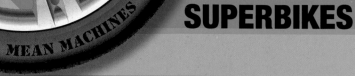

HONDA GOLDWING

Not all superbikes are about brash displays of power and high-speed thrills. The Honda Goldwing's approach is more laid back and luxurious. Welcome to the world of the super touring bike. These massive machines are designed for long-distance driving – with supreme style and comfort.

Touring bikes need to store a rider's baggage. The Goldwing has around 150 litres of storage space with areas in the saddlebags, boot and fairings.

The Honda Goldwing is the king of the touring bike world. These iconic bikes have been in production since 1975. They are built for carrying a rider plus a passenger. Now the bikes come packed with more creature comforts than ever before.

There's no danger of getting lost – the Goldwing comes complete with a built-in satellite navigation system.

You can listen to music on touring bikes. The Goldwing has surround sound speakers and you can play either mp3s or cds.

Over 640,000 Honda Goldwings have been sold so far.

There are heated seats and warm air vents for your feet.

The seats are adjustable for both the rider and passenger.

Touring bikes are big and heavy, so they use lots of fuel. The Goldwing uses about the same amount of fuel as a family car.

SUPER STATS

HONDA GL 1800 GOLDWING DELUXE

TOP SPEED: Not released
WEIGHT: 417 kg (919 lbs)
ENGINE: 118 bhp
MADE IN: Japan
PRICE: £23,125

HARLEY DAVIDSON DYNA SUPER GLIDE CUSTOM

Some superbikes are good for one thing in particular – showing off. If you're riding a bike that's really special, then you want other people to notice it. A good way of attracting attention is to customise your bike. This means adjusting the way it looks or rides. Manufacturers like Harley Davidson will do all the hard work for you.

The Super Glide doesn't use modern metals such as titanium to get a shine. Instead it uses old-fashioned chrome – just like they used to.

The paint on Harley Davidsons is twice as thick as other manufacturers'.

Riders can customise their Super Glide in all sorts of ways. The suspension can be adjusted, different seats can be bought and even the engine can be altered.

Harley Davidson is one of the most famous motorbike manufacturers in the world. This American company started building bikes in 1903 and was soon building iconic bikes that appealed to everyone from police forces to biker gangs. The Super Glide Custom is designed to look a little old fashioned to remind people of Harley's history.

The 'pullback' handlebars are comfortable to hold when cruising long distances.

All the gauges and instruments are positioned on the top of the fuel tank.

Customers can have anti-lock brakes if they want. These stop the wheels from locking if the bike slows down too quickly.

SUPER STATS

HARLEY DAVIDSON DYNA SUPER GLIDE CUSTOM
TOP SPEED: 185 km/h (115 mph)
WEIGHT: 294 kg (648 lbs)
ENGINE: 65 bhp
MADE IN: USA
PRICE: From £8,330

REWACO FX6

If you want a superbike that really gets you noticed, you might need a completely different sort of machine. And nothing is more guaranteed to cause stares than a supertrike. Vehicles such as the Rewaco FX6 prove that three-wheelers aren't just for toddlers!

Customers can order a top box for storage and can also get saddlebags.

Stable, powerful trikes such as the Rewaco can even tow a trailer or caravan.

The engine is made by the famous American motorcycle firm, Harley Davidson.

The FX6 has two seats, but up to four people can fit on some trikes.

The real advantage of trikes such as the Rewaco FX6 over bikes is that they are a lot more stable. Having three wheels means that you don't have to balance. So trike riders get all the feel and enjoyment of riding a motorbike – without the problem of falling off!

Lightness isn't really the top priority with the FX6, so there's lots of shiny chrome.

The FX6 might be heavy, but in can still get to 100 km/h (62 mph) in under 8 seconds!

The shock absorbers can be adjusted for a sporty or more comfortable ride.

The body of the trike is made of plastic reinforced with glass fibre.

SUPER STATS

REWACO FX6 1.6L
TOP SPEED: 156 km/h (97 mph)
WEIGHT: 530 kg (1168 lbs)
ENGINE: 85 bhp
MADE IN: Germany
PRICE: £25,000+

GLOSSARY

aluminium a lightweight metal

bhp This stands for 'brake horsepower', and is a measurement of the power of an engine.

carbon fibre a strong, light material made from thin rods of carbon. Carbon is also found in coal and diamonds.

chassis the base of a motor vehicle

concept a plan or idea

durable able to resist damage

exclusive available to a small group of people, and no one else

manufacturer the person or company that has made something

reinforce to make stronger

rigid able to stay the same shape, without bending

shale a soft type of rock made from layers of mud or clay

suspension the system in vehicles that stops passengers from feeling bumps

terrain the shape of an area of land, and the features of that area, such as trees

tribute an action that shows admiration for someone or something

FURTHER READING

Editors of QED. *Cars and Bikes (Machines at Work).* Kingscourt, 2007.

Gifford, Clive. *Extreme Motorbikes.* A&C Black, 2009.

Mason, Paul. *Bike Mechanic (Instant Expert).* A&C Black, 2011.

Oxlade, Chris. *Motorbikes (Extreme Machines).* Franklin Watts, 2009.

Parker, Steve. *How It Works: Cars, Trucks and Bikes.* Miles Kelly, 2009.

INDEX